12 EXPLOSIVE SECRETS

To

ELIMINATE STRESS AND CHANGE YOUR BRAIN

A COMPLETE GUIDE TO 12 PRINCIPLES THAT WILL ELIMINATE YOUR EVERYDAY STRESS, CHANGE YOUR MIND AND LIFE

Steve Meyer

Copyright © 2021 by Steve Meyer - All rights reserved.

The content contained within this book may not be reproduced, duplicated, or transmitted without direct written permission from the author or the publisher except for the use of brief quotations in a book review. Under no circumstances will any blame or legal responsibility be held against the publisher, or author, for any damages, reparation, or monetary loss due to the information contained within this book. Either directly or indirectly. You are responsible for your own choices, actions, and results.

Legal Notice:

This book is copyright protected. This book is only for personal use. You cannot amend, distribute, sell, use, quote or paraphrase any part, or the content within this book, without the consent of the author or publisher except for the use of brief quotations in a book review.

Disclaimer Notice:

Please note the information contained within this book is for educational and entertainment purposes only. All effort has been executed to "present accurate, up to date, and reliable, complete information. No warranties of any kind are declared or implied. Readers acknowledge that the author is not engaging in the rendering of legal, financial, medical, or professional advice. The content within this book has been derived from various sources. Please consult a licensed professional before attempting any techniques outlined in this book. By reading this book, the reader agrees that under no circumstances is the author responsible for any losses, direct or indirect, which are incurred as a result of the use of the information contained within this book, including, but not limited to, — errors, omissions, or inaccuracies."

Download Your Free Gift

Before you go any further, why not pick up a gift from us to you?

GROWTH PRINCIPLES

If you're willing to learn and transform yourself in all the right areas,

then success is definitely for you.

So, to find out how you can do that, let's get reading.

Scan the barcode to get it before it expires!

Table of Contents:

Introduction..3
Secret #1: Relaxation..11
Secret #2: Keep a Regular Exercise Schedule................................ 17
Secret #3: Try Some Meditation Techniques...................................22
Secret #4: Set Aside Time Every Day to Do Things You Enjoy........................31
Secret #5: Eat Right..38
Secret #6: Get Enough Sleep..42
Secret #7: Learn How Stress Affects the Body................................46
Secret #8: Have a Contingency Plan..54
Secret #9: Remember You've Been There Before...........................57
Secret #10: Listen to Music..60
Secret #11: Minimize Distractions...65
Secret #12: Call Someone..68
Conclusion..72

Introduction

In order to avoid stress overload, you'll need to make time for relaxation as well as exercise and stress relief techniques. Tickle your funny bone with a few jokes, take a deep breath or two before making a decision, or just find something that helps you feel more relaxed. You will feel better for it.

Stress management is an umbrella term used to describe any tactics that can help you cope with stress. The 12 Secrets for Stress Management you read about here are all techniques that can be employed with varying degrees of success, but all of these techniques will help you reduce the negative effects of stress. Keep reading for more on what stress does, strategies to prevent it, and even ways to use it in our favor.

What is Stress?

Stress is defined as being 'at tension' or being under pressure. When we are stressed, our body releases stress hormones that help us handle danger when you are running away from a predator or responding to an impending stressful event. That can be anything from an important deadline at work to making a speech in front of people, taking an exam, racing against time, etc.

Stress can be anything from a short lecture to a major social event. When you feel that you're under too much pressure, stress is the result. Feeling anxious and tense are indications of stress. If you think consistently about what a big deal a situation is, it's an indication that your emotions are being waylaid by stress. Stress is often described as a mental state where our bodies -- including our heart rate, breathing, and blood pressure -- produce stress hormones such as adrenaline and cortisol to help us cope with situations that may involve danger or uncertainty . Since the human body wasn't designed to stand up under stress 24/7, it's important to find ways to relax and relieve stress.

The Many Faces of Stress

Stress is an umbrella term that covers several emotions that aren't always easy to identify. When you're tense, stressed out, or anxious, you're feeling some combination of frustration, anger, anxiety, and fear. How stressed you are depends on how stressful your life is. If something is bothering you or making you mad every day at work, the stress will build over time until it becomes overwhelming. When it comes to managing stress , finding out what causes your irritability will help you reduce your overall stress level so you won't feel so bad all the time.

If you're dealing with stress , it's not always easy to identify the source because you're feeling a multitude of emotions at once. These multiple emotions may be causing the physical problems that stress causes. The best way to get rid of stress is by taking care of yourself so you can enjoy all your activities without having to worry about anything else.

Stress occurs when there are too many things going on in your life at once. If you're feeling overwhelmed, learn to prioritize the things your have to do and concentrate on each item one at a time. If you can't get rid of all your stress, you should at least try to reduce some of the problems in your life.

It's a common phrase, but one that needs to be repeated over and over again: successful people know how to manage their stress. And yet, too many people refuse to take it seriously.

In here, you'll learn what causes stress and what you can do about it—from the fundamental steps of relaxation techniques like meditation or deep breathing, all the way up to more advanced techniques like cognitive behavioral therapy (CBT).

For readers looking to relax, try the simple method in 'How to Relax' in this chapter.

There are two main types of stress:

Acute stress is our natural response to a specific event or series of events, typically an emotional reaction.

Chronic stress is the body's physical and emotional response to prolonged work pressure, preoccupation or trauma that occurs for weeks, months or years.

When we talk about stress management techniques, we're usually talking about helping people deal with acute and chronic stressors in their lives. Ideally, it would be great if everyone could manage their acute stressors without any help from a professional—but the truth is most people need outside help from time to time.

The main idea behind stress management is that you can decrease the impact of stress by learning how to think and act in response to it. The thing about stressors, though, is that they're similar to physical pain: there's no way for you to control them directly. But what you can do is approach them, change your thoughts and feelings about them, and apply other strategies for coping with stressful situations.

In fact, one of the most important aspects of stress management is understanding the psychology behind what makes you stressed out. Once you know why a certain situation affects you adversely, then you can work on ways to prevent that situation from negatively affecting your emotions and thoughts.

As we go through this, I'm going to continually talk about our reactions being affected by the way we process events in our brain. The good news is that if we understand how we psychologically respond to things, then we can work on changing those automatic patterns and make better decisions under pressure. Let's talk about the three different frames of mind that cause us to respond in unhealthy ways to stressful events.

The Three Key Frameworks in Stress Management

Subconscious vs. Conscious Mind

There are three main elements that contribute to your mindset when it comes to responding to stressors. The first one is the subconscious, or "non-conscious," mind, which is a fancy way of saying that we don't have direct control over the thoughts and feelings that pop into our heads. This part of your mind is always working behind the scenes—and it doesn't necessarily work in your favor when faced with a stressor.

For example, when you encounter a stressor, your automatic response will be based on the fears and worries you developed when you were younger. These are passive thoughts that don't require any effort on your part to form—they just happen when you're in the right set of circumstances.

Think about it like this: when faced with an acutely stressful situation, there's a good chance that a large amount of this nervousness is unintentional and has nothing to do with you. It's why it's so important to do everything in your power to make sure the situations you put yourself in don't upset your mind.

The second part of your mindset is the conscious mind, which you have the most control over. When you're being consciously mindful, you're being aware of what's happening around you—and that's something anyone can achieve with practice. This involves taking steps to change your thoughts and feelings so that they are in line with what you want to accomplish in life.

For example, if you have a chronic issue at work that's making you stressed out, it's important to be aware of your emotional state every day when you get home from work. Do you feel a rush of adrenaline after pushing through another workday? Are you dealing with a bad mood or an anxiety attack? By consciously monitoring your emotions, you can make sure that the stress is getting better—or at least not affecting you as badly.

Consciousness vs. Unconscious Mind

When we're talking about stress management, the third part of the mindset comes into play: conscious awareness. The goal here is to be aware of your thoughts and feelings around a stressful event and take steps to change them, so that other emotional patterns don't come out and become automatic.

This is where most people fail (or don't even realize they're doing it). What most people do is get into the state of mind that I call "automatic pilot." This happens when you don't pay attention to your thoughts or feelings, and your physical reactions to stressors are merely a result of this.

Automated Stress Management

When we're in automatic pilot, we're not having conscious control over how we feel or think; instead, the subconscious becomes the dominant element in our mindset. This combination of our non-conscious and conscious thoughts can make it very difficult for us to make good decisions—particularly when the stakes are high (which is usually everything in life).

Here are three of the most common automatic reaction patterns that lead to chronic stress:

The "Fight or Flight" Response The "Shut Down" Response The "Defuse with Humor" Response

The "Fight or Flight" Response is our physical reaction to stressors. For example, if you're stressed out because you're stuck working on an assignment at work with no end in sight, your body will respond by telling your brain to flee from the situation—to get away from it, so that it doesn't have to deal with the situation anymore. This physical response can also happen when we're afraid of something and we subconsciously choose to be fearful rather than brave.

The "Shut Down" Response is different than the "Fight or Flight" response. When we're stressed out, our body will create the same sense of fear that comes with the "Fight or Flight" response—but instead of acting on that fear, we shut down and choose to do nothing about it. This is the result of believing that the stressor is too big for you to deal with at once.

The "Defuse with Humor" Response happens when we subconsciously decide to find something funny about a stressful situation. For example, you've got a big presentation coming up at work, and you feel completely stressed out. Instead of taking appropriate steps to deal with your stress, you just tell yourself that the stress makes you "hilarious." If you're lucky, this type of humor helps alleviate some of the fear and anxiety—but it's not healthy.

When we're in automatic electric, our minds are most likely trying to protect us from the effects of an intense stressor—but by doing so, it can make things worse.

How are you dealing with stress?

Most of us are not aware that our conscious mind is "supposed" to be the one doing all of the work. Under stress, we usually rely on our subconscious mode of thinking, which means that we're dragging our conscious into an unhealthy place where it doesn't belong. We may even think that the problem isn't actually in us—that it's in the situation. Instead of taking action to change things, though, people merely suffer when faced with a chronic stressful situation.

But by using mindful awareness in your day-to-day life, you can put yourself at ease when things get stressful so that your subconscious actions become more healthy ones. You can't control all the stressors that you face in life, but you can take refuge in the fact that you can be alert to them and recognize what they're doing to your body.

When you become aware, instead of shutting down or going into a frenzy, you have a chance to embrace a different response—one that will help you live better.

How do you REACT?

The sooner we realize this, the sooner we can begin healing from it! If your stress levels are high and you're noticing an impact on your health and happiness, start making small changes that could help bring those stress levels down.

Start by resting more.

Get moving.

Secret #1: Relaxation

Many people who suffer from stress and/or anxiety find that relaxation techniques, such as meditation and yoga, can help manage their symptoms. They introduce a sense of calm to your life. But you need not take time out of your day for the sake of these techniques — deep breathing is something you can do anywhere at any time. It's free and it's convenient! This relaxation technique can put an end to racing thoughts, slow your heart rate, and even lower blood pressure!

Breathing exercises such as this one are a great way to relax and destress! You can do it anywhere and it makes you feel better almost immediately.. We hope you'll give deep breathing a try!

When you find that certain activities help relieve stress or tension better than others, then those should be your go-to methods. This is an example of how different methods can work for different people.

For instance, if you get a massage, you might get an immediate release from the tension in your muscles. You then might notice that you're able to think more clearly and creatively for a short period of time. However, you may not be able to get this same benefit from other forms of relaxation. It's also possible that a different activity might help you feel more relaxed longer-term without the "high" sensation that comes from a massage or other similar activity.

You can find numerous methods of reducing stress and improving the quality of your life. Here are just a few of them:

When you first want to relax, it's best to start with simple things that are easy for you. Simple things like taking a bath, washing your face, or reading a book may help ease stress and tension enough for you to take time out to relax without too much trouble. The more difficult activities should be reserved for your 'best' relaxing days or times. If you are having trouble getting certain things done, then these are the activities that should be the focus of your efforts.

- Deep breaths are one of the best ways to relieve tension and stress because breathing deeply will provide oxygen throughout your body and mind. This is a good way to release tension in your muscles and throughout your entire body.

- Try listening to music. One study found that listening to music can be used as a form of relaxation for both school children and adults. Students were asked to listen to music while they did their schoolwork - and it worked well for them! Adults were also able to relieve stress and tension by listening to certain songs while they did housework - including ironing! The two main benefits of listening to music while relaxing are that it can help block outside noise and it's easier on your brain than many other forms of relaxation.

- Visualization is a simple and effective way to relax and relieve stress and tension. When you visualize yourself in a relaxing scenario, you are likely to feel calmer simply because you are focusing on things that make you happy. It's important to find whatever works best for you - for example, visualizing yourself at the beach with the sun shining down on you or floating away on a cloud can be very powerful if it works for you. If imagining yourself in your own home helps, then by all means do that!

- Aromatherapy is an easy way to relax by using certain scents that are known to reduce stress levels. Find an aromatherapy product that you find soothing by visiting this site. Many of the products are natural, non-toxic, and are packaged for convenience.

- Massage is another form of relaxation therapy that can be very beneficial when done right. The right massage therapist can use their hands, words, or even their body to help relieve stress in your muscles by touching them in the right spots. This book allows you to find the right massage therapist for yourself.

- A hot bath can provide a relaxing effect that lasts for quite some time. The water can also help you relieve stress, which is useful if you suffer from this condition. Not only is the bath easy on your muscles, it can be used to help relax other parts of your body as well. So if you are experiencing joint pain, for instance, soaking in a tub might make it easier to be rid of this problem.

- Stretching out in bed is one of the easiest ways to relax your body because it involves very little effort on your part. You might want to try this out if you have a hard time shutting off your mind before going to sleep.

- Writing down your thoughts and feelings is one of the best ways to relieve stress and tension that builds up from your day-to-day activities. It can be very stressful to constantly be on the go without stopping to take a look at what's causing the stress, dealing with it, and possibly learning from it. Be sure to use a notebook or journal so that you don't have to worry about losing what you've written.

- If moving around reduces stress for you then try dancing or jogging outside. If relaxing with an animal is your style then get a cat or dog! They're always happy to see you and don't mind getting some cuddles from auntie while they're at it (not that I would know anything about that). If you're looking for high quality pet care for your furry friend, please feel free to contact me.

- Celebrate Yourself -Celebrate the person you are because giving yourself credit where it's due is quite enjoyable. Maybe eating ice cream sounds like a great way to end the day - who cares what others say?

- Be Aware of Your Limitations - You can't do everything all at once. You have limitations and you should be aware of them. Use them to your advantage by knowing when to back off, give yourself permission to chill out, or take a break if necessary. Don't worry about falling behind - life won't stop just because you don't keep up with it anymore.

- Make Music - Does listening to music calm you down? Maybe there's a way you can create some! Writing songs or poetry is a great way to express yourself...and it doesn't have to be "the great American novel".

...And if none of these things appeal to you, then do something completely different! Here are some suggestions:

- Try gardening. Find out what grows in your area and watch them turn into beautiful flowers.

- Take some time away from technology - Get out of the house or office and go somewhere new.

- Go to the beach - just try it. It might help to go somewhere quiet and relax your mind - maybe you'll meet up with an old friend there.

If you'd like some advice on what to do, feel free to contact me! I've got some ideas...I just need to know first if you're interested!

So there you have it, folks. That's quite enough of that stress-relief stuff for now. Instead though, here are six tips for helping you relax at the end of the day:

1. Don't panic

2. Don't stress

3. Relax your body

4. Ask yourself what's stressing you, then analyse it rationally to see if it's worth worrying about (and if not, just forget about it)

5. If you're still stressed, try talking to someone. It'll help you to relieve some of that pent-up emotion and take your mind off of your problems for a while. However, don't talk about your problems 24/7...or your friends might get bored.

6. Help someone else. You can't change the world all by yourself...but if everyone helps one person, things will get done! That's the whole point of this chapter; to make you feel better. And I really hope that it does. So take your time now, and click on whatever interests you the most (in case you got here by accident).

Secret #2: Keep a Regular Exercise Schedule

Exercise is one of the most effective ways to reduce stress and keep it away for good.

Stress, the kind that makes you feel sick when it's too much is linked with a number of medical conditions. It's important to choose activities that challenge yourself in some way so that you remain healthy and satisfied.

While stress can sometimes be a wonderful motivator for getting up in the morning, it can also become a huge source of exhaustion. With this in mind, you have to find a way to not let your stress levels get out of hand if they start affecting your day-to-day life.

Doing something that you enjoy will help ease the pressure that you feel when you're constantly being reminded of all of your responsibilities and challenges. If yoga is not your thing, feel free to pick up a new sport or join a gym! A study done by the University of Southern California showed that physical activities such as exercise and sports improve cognitive function significantly.

If keeping your mind sharp is what you want, be sure to incorporate in some activity that will challenge and stretch your muscles and mind in a powerful way.

Pick a sport that you're interested in, and be sure to give it a try! You might also try joining a gym or fitness center if the sport isn't for you.

If your fitness is focused more on building muscle or weight loss, you might find that a gym is the best option. You'll be able to keep up with your goals and remain healthy while doing so!

Exercise and sports can also help with anxiety and depression. This is because they require thinking and movement, which releases chemicals in your brain associated with feelings of happiness. It can even help improve cognitive function on its own even without exercise! This is because exercise increases the flow of blood to the brain, helping it stay alert and thinking clearly. These results can be seen when you combine regular exercise with cognitive therapy.

This type of therapy is recommended for those who are struggling to reach their health goals. They work by helping you identify the root cause of your issues and focus on ways to change it. It's important to find a therapist that will be able to make it work for your schedule!

Leaving work early once in a while is also an option. Remember, there are tons of great activities out there that are free or cheap! You'll be able to focus more on being active rather than on having enough money for the latest workout craze. This means that you're likely to avoid making excuses about why you can't go to your favorite gym because it's too expensive, too far away, too crowded, etc.

Fitness doesn't have to be a full-time job, or even something that you do everyday! It's all about finding an activity that will get your blood pumping for an hour or so while helping you relax! You may not even have to spend money or take up tons of your free time. You can even use the social media that you may already be using with your friends or family to get in shape!

Whether you're completely new at working out or would like to add more variety to your fitness routine, there is something for everyone. Keep in mind that many Americans spend a third of their day sitting down, which leaves less time for movement and physical activity. If it's important for you to stay healthy and fit, set aside some extra time in your day so that you have the chance to build a solid routine for yourself! Try going on a hike after work one week and do a yoga session the next!

Now that we've covered the basics of setting up a fitness routine, we can now look at some more advanced tips that will help you truly feel the benefits of exercise and experiment with new exercises. I'll be honest: not everyone enjoys working out, and sometimes people choose to push themselves to the limit and push themselves beyond their limits so they don't have to work out.

While this kind of behavior is admirable it has its downsides as well. If you pass out on the trail or trail of your workout, you'll have done more harm than good. Not only can exercise be severely detrimental to your overall health, but it can put a damper on your social life as well. As far as fitness is concerned, the two key ingredients are balance and moderation.

Instead of leaving yourself with no downtime at all, choose to do an activity that will leave you feeling invigorated and relaxed. These are very helpful in working out the body's core muscles and leaving you feeling content.

Not everyone has the same end goals when it comes to fitness. While you may want to drop 30 pounds off your hips or thighs, someone else might be looking for a good workout tool for strength training or weight loss. This will help you avoid disappointing yourself, and it might even make you feel like you're accomplishing something!

Whether it's yoga for flexibility, weights for weight loss or pilates for toning up your core muscles, there are plenty of options to find the right one for you. There are so many great videos out there with so many different exercises in them.

Some people are naturally flexible while others need to work on their flexibility through yoga! Whatever your goals might be, you can easily find a type of fitness that will help you achieve them. While some may opt for simple exercises that are enjoyable, others may want to push themselves with weight lifting techniques or even try using resistance bands for their flexibility training!

Look out for muscle soreness, pain and even fatigue. If you're working out in a gym, talk to the staff about how to avoid injuries and health problems. These people are professionals and will be able to give you great advice based on your fitness level!

Don't be afraid to ask for help either; whether it's from friends, fitness enthusiasts or even your doctor. Not only can this help keep you in good health but it will also help prevent injury and keep you safe in general. After all, if you're injured you can't work out.

It's also important to make sure your fitness routine is sustainable. If it's something that you don't like too much, or that you feel like it's bringing you down, then try something else! There are hundreds of different ways you can exercise and there is no one way that will work for everyone!

The most vital thing though is to find a fitness routine that works for you and your needs.

Secret #3: Try Some Meditation Techniques

When faced with the stress of life, it is important not to forget that your mind is running your life. Luckily, meditation techniques can be practiced and mastered to help you manage and eliminate stress. This chapter will teach you how to meditate and integrate these tools into your daily routine.

Meditation Techniques to Eliminate Stress:

This will discuss the benefits of meditation as well as different ways in which people could approach this practice for effective relief from anxiety and depression. As far back as recorded history goes, man has been learning techniques such as sitting mediation or walking meditation to reduce high levels of anxiety or relieve depression. Modern medical studies have shown that these practices actually work. You don't have to have a doctorate in medicine to recognize the benefits. If you are struggling with stress, meditating is your best shot at eliminating it completely.

The Benefits of Meditation:

One of the greatest benefits of meditation is that it allows you to calm your mind. When your mind is not distracted by anxiety it can be easily focused on something you truly want, like improving your skills at playing the piano or learning how to speak another language. It's known as "mindfulness" or simply "being present." You may choose to meditate standing up or seated, depending on what is most comfortable for you.

Meditation Techniques to Control Stress:

The most important thing to remember is that meditation is not a religion. It doesn't require you to believe in anything whatsoever. The only requirement for meditation is that you are actually doing it. If you are using meditation as a way to escape reality, or as a way of filling up time, well, the opposite of what it was "meant" for you to be doing. If you are looking for techniques to reduce anxiety and eliminate stress, there are several different ways you can practice this practice. The key to success with any type of meditation is consistency. If you can find time to fit meditation in every day, you will be much better off in the long run.

These meditation techniques can be used during any moment in your day when you feel stressed or anxious. The key is to "be in the moment" rather than somewhere else in your mind. Try breathing deeply, and concentrate on your breath.

The goal of these types of mediation techniques is simply to bring your mind back into focus by calming it down from all of the distractions. In order for these meditations to work effectively, you have to be able to fully concentrate on what is going on around you at that particular time that you are practicing it. In other words, "be present."

Meditation is a wonderful way to relieve stress and calm your mind.
It is important to remember that you must be patient and consistent. Don't expect to see results overnight. Training your mind with this practice takes time, practice, and patience.
If you are looking for meditation techniques to reduce stress, you can do so by simply withdrawing yourself from all distractions. If you are constantly being pulled in other directions by the various issues life has set out before you, then it will be much harder for you to achieve these goals. When practicing mindfulness meditation techniques , have the patience not to get too distracted because this will only hinder your progress even more. The first step is learning how to focus. Once you learn how to shut out the distractions, you'll be able to reach "the zone" of meditation. There are more advanced techniques like "walking meditation" or "mindfulness meditation." These are more advanced techniques get started with basic sitting or standing meditations, but do what is most comfortable for you.

Mindfulness Meditation Techniques:

The purpose of mindfulness meditation is to simply focus on your breathing and nothing else. The more you can focus on your breathing, the less likely you will be distracted by other thoughts that might cause anxiety or distraction. For example, it's easy to become very anxious when looking at bills that need to be written about. Instead of looking at the bills, just take a moment to focus on your breathing. This is only one way to meditate, but it will help you calm down and reach that inner peace that is just out of view.

Mindfulness meditation techniques are all about learning to control your attention.
For instance, if you find yourself becoming anxious about talking to someone new, don't let the anxiety get the best of you. Instead, stop for a moment and focus on your breathing. You might notice how each breath comes in through the nose only and forces itself out through the mouth.
This is not something you can do during regular conversation, but it can be practiced when talking with someone new.

Walking Meditation Techniques:

These walking meditation techniques are very similar to standing meditation except you are walking. This is a great way to increase stress relief if anxiety is causing problems with your sleep.
It's better to practice walking meditation in the afternoon or evening, or of course, during waking hours. It's important to not try walking meditation during early morning because this will usually interrupt your sleep cycle.
If you are trying to fall asleep at night, try practicing seated meditation instead of walking meditation.

When we talk about breathing we usually associate it with our lungs and how much oxygen we breathe in and out. However, breathing means more than that. It also refers to the movement of air that our body makes.

For example, when we inhale (inhale=in=to fill), the air goes up the nostrils and fills the lungs. When we exhale (exhale=ex=out it causes air to be released from the lungs and goes out of our nose or eardrums.
For people who experience anxiety, they tend to have abnormal breathing patterns which worsen stress because their minds are worried about what will happen next. While this is a normal part of life, it may cause stress to become overwhelming for people who are prone to anxiety.

The quickest way to calm down and clear your mind is by taking deep breaths. However, take into account that these breathing techniques can cause you to become hyperventilating if done too quickly. Here's how to do it correctly:
Breathe in as deeply as possible so that your abdomen expands as much as possible.
Hold the breath for a few seconds, and then release it.
Repeat this process until you feel calm enough. This might take a couple of minutes or longer.

Many people find that at times their mind is filled with negative thoughts that keep sticking around and ruining a good day. While there are many ways to try and get rid of these negative thoughts, one of the best ways is through meditation. By meditating, you allow yourself to take the time to focus on all of your thoughts and emotions. This gives you the chance to recognize these thoughts and examine them in depth.
Another great reason why meditation is so effective with stress management is because it makes it easier for you to recognize your feelings. By doing this, you can then act accordingly. For example, if you are feeling scared or alone, then it's okay to take the time to relax and unwind.

Our body can be compared to a machine in many ways. Just like a machine, your body needs to be well maintained in order to work properly. When you practice meditation, you are able to keep the parts of your body in good working condition by minimizing stress. If you are able to eliminate stressful thoughts, then your lungs will have more room to provide you with enough oxygen.
By being able to relax during meditation, it gives us the chance to become more aware of our inner self. By becoming more aware of what makes us happy or sad, then we can do all that we can do in order not to have these negative emotions in the future.

Your body is a valuable part of your meditation because it can help you meditate more effectively over time. By being able to eliminate unnecessary stress from your body, you can help prevent many unwanted diseases from developing.

When we talk about the mind, we usually refer to it as one thing. In fact, our mind is capable of doing so many things that it would take a lot of time to write all the different functions down on paper. For example, our mind allows us to think freely, make decisions and feel emotions all in the same moment in time. It's important for us to understand that these three categories are strictly separate; however they are linked in some ways too. For example, making the decision to feel a certain way can sometimes cause us to think in a certain way. In general, it's good for us if we can establish a healthy mind so that we can have positive thoughts when we need to. As for our emotions, these are what keep us going when times get tough. For this reason, it's important that you learn how to control your emotions so that you will be able to lead an easier life.

It is extremely important for you to be able to recognize your own thoughts and emotions. If you are unable to identify what makes you feel the way that you do, then it will be harder for people with anxiety or depression to treat their symptoms effectively.

It is known that our brains can be divided into two separate parts: the left and right hemispheres. The two hemispheres also have separate functions: The left side of the brain is used for logic, rational thinking, and details. On the other hand, the right side of the brain is used for creativity, intuition, and emotions. By now you probably guessed that the left hemisphere is used for negative thinking while the right hemisphere focuses on positive aspects. An important thing to understand is that your emotions do not control your thoughts. Sometimes people will start having negative thoughts which causes an emotional response to follow suit.

Your body will thank you if you are able to eliminate stress more efficiently. One of the most effective ways to relieve stress is through meditation. However, you need to make sure that you do it correctly because it can cause some health problems if done incorrectly. Meditation is a great way for people with depression and anxiety to get rid of their negative thoughts. By being able to recognize all of your thoughts, then you will be able to keep them from becoming overwhelming. In effect, this will allow people who have depression or anxiety from overreacting while working towards managing their symptoms. If you are going to meditate properly, then it's a good idea to read more about the topic so that you can learn how it can benefit your stress levels.

A great way to get rid of stress is through meditation. When we speak about meditation, we usually mean the act of focusing on your breathing and thoughts. This can be done in a few different ways: Breathing in and out: Breathing in and out will help you to focus on your breathing. Through this type of meditation, you can allow yourself to learn how to control your thoughts. Chanting: Chanting is a form of meditation that lets you focus on your breathing patterns. Visualization: By visualizing an object, such as a tree or the sun, then the object will help you to calm down.

There are many different ways to meditate. You can learn how to do this by listening to a guided meditation audio. This will allow you the time to take all of your thoughts and focus on them so that you can eliminate the ones that stress your body and mind.
Another great thing about meditation is that it helps us better understand ourselves and our emotions. As we get older we tend to put up a bunch of walls around us in order not to be hurt by negative thoughts and feelings. When we start taking down these walls, then we start becoming more aware of who we really are.

When we think of our feelings, we usually picture a specific emotion. For example, you might picture a feeling of love, anger, or sadness. Since we can't see our emotions at any given time, it seems as if the only way to know what they are is to experience them. When we focus on our feelings throughout the day, then this change in perspective will allow us to learn how to control them. There are many different ways that you can relate these feelings and emotions with your inner self. For example: You can focus on how you feel about yourself and the actions that you take every day. This helps us to gain an understanding of what we want from life and what we need - both internally and externally.

Whenever you start to feel stressed or frustrated, then it's a good idea to meditate. As we mentioned previously, these moments cause your body to feel a little bit of pain. By being able to use a few techniques to relax yourself, then you can minimize these negative emotions so that they don't have as big of an impact on your well being.

If you want other people to understand what your feeling, then it's best not be so vague with the words that you use. People will have a better understanding of how you feel if they can actually picture what is going through your mind because this usually leads them towards feelings of empathy and sadness.

It's very important if you want people to pay attention and listen to what you're saying. At times it may be difficult for you to talk about what is going on inside of your body, but by learning how to do this properly, then this will help you in the long run.

Secret #4: Set Aside Time Every Day to Do Things You Enjoy

If you have a hobby, spend some time doing it.

If you're feeling overwhelmed and frazzled, we've got some good news: research shows that taking time away from the stress of work every day can actually lower your stress levels. In fact, a recent study found that people who participate in low-stress activities for even just 5 minutes a day end up with lower average stress levels.

In order to take back control of your life from all the stressful things going on outside, make a point to set aside time every day to do something you enjoy. It does not matter if it is taking a walk outdoors, listening to music, playing with your pet, just enjoy. It really doesn't matter what you do as long as you give yourself some time to do something that makes you happy.

Stressed people will often find themselves doing three things rather than one: work more hours, isolate themselves further from others, and eat more junk food.

All of these behaviors can lead to weight gain and many problems associated with general stress load including cardiovascular disease, diabetes or even depression. To manage stress effectively there needs to be some time available for enjoyable activities that are free from distractions.

If you become a master of the office, but don't enjoy anything outside of work, you will burn out, which can be at least as stressful as what was going on in the office. Find a balance between work and play to help prevent this from happening. If you already have a difficult time finding time to do things you enjoy, try carving out 5 minutes a day to do something that makes you happy. You may find that it is easier than expected. If not, allow yourself 10 minutes or 1/2 an hour every day to enjoy some light-hearted recreation.

Five minutes is the perfect amount of time to participate in an activity that can help get your blood flowing and reduce stress levels. The recent study found that people who participated in activities such as dancing, socializing and meditation (1) reduced their stress levels by up to 30 percent. For most people 5 minutes is more than enough time, but you can also try for 10 minutes if you wish.

How often should I find the spare time to do something I enjoy?

You can exercise almost anytime; we've discussed many times how much better your health and fitness will be when you incorporate exercise into your daily routine. However, you want to make sure that exercise has a relaxing effect because not all exercises are equally effective at lowering stress levels when done too vigorously. You want to make sure that you are not damaged your body or tired yourself out during strenuous exercise. If you find yourself becoming stressed out from time to time, take a break from exercise and go take a walk outside for a little bit.

One of the easiest ways to address stress is by finding an enjoyable activity that you can just do as a separate endeavor from work. This type of activity is extremely important if you work in an office job, as all the research has shown that people who just have their own single-tasking pantry jobs create more stressful jobs for themselves because they take on much more stress than those who have a well-balanced lifestyle overall.

It's important that whatever you choose to do, you enjoy it and like to do it, otherwise you may end up spending time doing something that isn't very fun. Granted, you could force yourself to feel better by doing something that makes you unhappy, but this will likely not be a long-term solution and will make things worse in the long run. So choose something like:

(1) Listening to music – Whether it's classical, jazz or rock and roll; listening to music is a great way to help relax your mind and body. Feel free to dance as well! One study found that dancing is as effective as yoga for reducing stress levels.

(2) Dancing – Dancing seems like a silly activity to include in this list, but do not underestimate the benefits of starting fun movements that are cool in themselves. Start with something easy like the chicken dance or then move on to forms that are more complex when you feel ready. Dancing can help reduce blood pressure, improve

your self-esteem, increase energy levels and improve your mood in general because it causes changes in heart rate, blood pressure and brain waves. The best thing about dancing is that you have the ability to enjoy the moment, have fun and forget about everything else.

– Dancing seems like a silly activity to include in this list, but do not underestimate the benefits of starting fun movements that are cool in themselves. Start with something easy like the chicken dance or then move on to forms that are more complex when you feel ready. Dancing can help reduce blood pressure, improve your self-esteem, increase energy levels and improve your mood in general because it causes changes in heart rate, blood pressure and brain waves. The best thing about dancing is that you have the ability to enjoy the moment, have fun and forget about everything else. Relaxation – Related to dancing is the need for a good stress relief program.

If you have other people who influence your actions, it's important to be aware of what is going on with them as well. If you have other friends or family members who are stressed out as well, it may be time to get everyone together to try something fun as a group. If you have a spouse or significant other, you may have to ask them for some time alone, otherwise it will be hard to find time for anything else. Stress starts on a personal level and it is important that individuals take responsibility on their own so they can be proactive on how to manage their stress levels.

What should I do if I have more work-related stress than play-related stress?

If you find yourself being consumed with work and having little activity outside of work all the time, then you may need to make some changes. However, the first step is to actively seek out solutions that will help reduce your stress levels. Although you can't control everything that happens in your life, you can control the way that you react to your life.

Most people will feel like they don't have time for fun, but if they looked closer at their schedule, they would see there is enough time to get the job done and also get some relaxation in. You should aim to take short breaks or longer breaks around mid-day for around 10 minutes to 1/2 an hour. This gives your body a chance to relax and resets your brain too, giving you more mental energy for the rest of the day.

Take the time to plan ahead about what you are going to do when taking breaks too. It's easy to say you will take a short break, but then you get busy with something else or have an interruption in your break. On paper, it may seem like only a few minutes have passed when in reality, it is much more than that if you took multiple breaks throughout the day. I recommend making notes in your smartphone or planner so that you know when each break will take place. Also, thinking ahead and working out what you will do when you get to each break can help you stay more organized and on point with the time of your day.

To help reduce stress levels while at work, try some of these suggestions:

Take some short breaks, at least 10 minutes each

Implement a regular lunch hour that you take every day. You need to get out of the office and away from your desk. Having an organized lunch break gives you some time to take care of yourself and also has been shown to help reduce stress levels. (3) If possible, go outside for a walk during your lunch break. You will feel better for it!

Don't forget to eat healthy during your lunch hour too. It is easy to get caught up in the busyness of life and make poor food choices when not paying attention.

Schedule in some fun time into your weekly schedule, no matter how little time you think you have. Maybe it's taking 20 minutes each week with friends after work, or maybe it's taking 20 minutes each day when things aren't as busy to relax and chill out a bit. Even if you only have 15 minutes each day, try to schedule it in and take advantage of it.

Take a break from work-related emails one day a week to check your personal email. If you do not have the time to break from work, then at least leave your computer open or critical emails that need critical attention open for this period of time.

If working long hours is causing stress, then seek out help to help reduce stress levels. You can talk to your boss about this or you can talk to someone outside of work. Hiring a life coach is a great way to help you calm down, focus on what is important and move life forward in a positive direction.

What if I am part of the problem with the amount of stress I put others under?

If you are someone who causes stress levels to rise in other people, then you have to take time out for yourself too. Even if that means setting an example for others that it's okay to take care of themselves by taking time out for themselves once in awhile. You can be better by being the first person to step up and say "I need some rest".

If you work in the healthcare industry, make a point to take a few days off each month. It can be a good thing for your own health along with the other people who depend on you as their healthcare provider as well as how it will improve the morale of your staff as well.

It's not just about taking time out for yourself, but also about helping those around you to take time out too. If those around you are stressed out or exhausted, then trying to solve that problem may cause more problems than it would solve. Instead, try and plan ahead and help others take active steps towards fixing their own stress levels and not yours.

Secret #5: Eat Right

Consumption of sugar and processed food leads to obesity, which leads to other health problems such as heart disease and diabetes, which can all increase your stress levels. Stay away from foods containing high fructose corn syrup and trans fats as much as possible.

Working hard and leading a full life can be draining. In fact, some research suggests that some people might experience more stress from work than from anything else in their lives.

The first step is to eliminate processed foods from your diet. Many people eat these because they are low-cost and convenient, but they actually contain unnecessary additives, chemicals, artificial flavors and toxic preservatives. These compounds actually work to increase your stress levels by deceiving your body into thinking it needs to produce more adrenaline. An elevated heart rate, muscle tension, and even headaches or migraines might result from this. High-fat foods such as fried foods and lard, on the other hand, should be avoided. While these may taste good (and maybe even help you relax), they can actually increase blood pressure and cause higher levels of cholesterol in the body.

Carbohydrates should also be at the top of your list. While they are not inherently stressful, too much can be. Foods like bread, rice, pasta and starchy vegetables like potatoes all contain simple sugars that can increase blood pressure and create a spike in glucose levels. This sudden rise in glucose can actually cause your adrenal glands to release more stress chemicals into the body.

When it comes to protein, there is no lack of variety out there. The natural proteins found in meats and seafood are actually very effective at reducing the amount of stress chemicals in the body like cortisol. This is because they supply you with amino acids along with any other vitamins or minerals that your body may need.

You may feel less worried and healthier than ever before with just a little effort!

The importance of eating right to eliminate stress has been an incredibly popular topic over the last few decades. In comparison to their thinner peers, the majority of clinically obese people are currently depressed, according to a new study. That is why it is critical for everyone to understand what foods to consume and avoid in order to reduce stress.

Depression is no longer a disorder that only affects high school aged teenagers. Now everyone from all walks of life can be susceptible to depression, even those who seem to have an adequate support system and should be at a low risk for depression.

Researchers speculate that the reason for this severe increase in depression cases has been attributed to the rise in obesity levels. In fact, obesity levels have skyrocketed within the past few years and research proves that this directly relates to the increase in major depressive disorders diagnosed every year.

The overwhelming increase of obesity rates has caused a direct impact on the condition of mental health as well as an increase in antidepressant prescriptions. According to a study completed by the American College of Physicians, nearly 20 million Americans take some form of psychiatric medication on a daily basis. And those who are obese tend to be more likely to be treated with antidepressants than those who are not. Even if this is not true for everyone, it is imperative that you understand your particular risk factors and how they may relate to your mental health and depression.

Oftentimes, there are things that we know will benefit our overall health but we do not do them because we assume that they are too extreme or a little too out of the ordinary. While some people may think that eating a diet that is high in protein and low in carbohydrates is extreme, it actually does have some very great benefits to help you eliminate your stress from your life.

In this study, researchers found that the majority of obese individuals who were suffering from depression had significantly lower levels of tryptophan than their thinner counterparts. In general, tryptophan is a type of amino acid that helps produce melatonin while also being a precursor to melatonin for melatonin receptors.

It has been established that daily melatonin production is optimal when around 200 mg of tryptophan is metabolized into serotonin. Tryptophan can also be used to produce the sleep hormone norepinephrine and anodine. Lastly, it can also be used to make a chemical called kynurenic acid which is non-essential in the body but has been found to have important anti-inflammatory properties.

Secret #6: Get Enough Sleep

You're tired. You're stressed. Your days are being ruined more often than not by the lack of sleep you are getting. Things worsen just when you believe they can't get much worse. You've gone from being a little bit out of it to feeling downright miserable, struggling just to get through your day at work or school...to getting some sleep. Who feels like this?

You can't seem to find enough time to rest, no matter how hard you try or how fatigued you are. You're tired, but first, you need to catch up on some things first. Sleeping is first on the list.

Why Sleep Makes Us Stressed

A lack of sleep is one of the major causes of stress in our lives. Our bodies were not meant to live without it. Sleep is essential for our energy, mood, and physical well-being.

Sleeping is a natural phenomenon that can't be fought. However, according to experts, we have become accustomed to sleeping less and less as years go on. Whereas once we might have taken a nap in the afternoon to make up for the sleep we missed the previous night, now people are going to bed at 10:00 or 11:00 pm on most nights and not getting up until around 8:00 or 9:00 am. In some cultures, these hours are even later. The result of this habit-breaking pattern is that people are simply not getting as much sleep as they need or can benefit from.

Sleep affects our moods, our productivity, our ability to concentrate and learn, solve problems creatively and master new tasks. Sleeps benefits are so well documented that there are many sleep clinics around the globe.

Relying on stimulants or staying awake too long simply because we become used to getting by on less sleep does not make up for what we've lost in terms of performance in school or at work. But the problem is that when we try to go back to catching up on sleep, it causes an even greater strain on our bodies. The mind wants rest, but when it needs rest it won't let us relax unless we recognize that need for what it is - a warning sign that something is wrong within us.

Getting Enough Sleep to Eliminate Stress

If you can't seem to get enough sleep and your life is a succession of restless nights, the first step is to admit that your position is untenable. The mind cannot function well if the body lacks proper sleep. When we fail to get the sleep we need, we learn that our bodies are not functioning properly or feel our jobs and responsibilities are too heavy for us.

If this is not you, then you may be able to get by with missing a few days here and there, but it's important to note that your brain will begin to crave sleep at some point and it won't be able to function if it doesn't receive sufficient rest. If you are finding that you can't get enough sleep because of your work schedule or lifestyle, then you may want to consider adjusting the things that are most important to you.

You have to decide if getting less sleep is really worth it. Even though being productive is your top goal at times, it is feasible to do so in a way that is less stressful on your body. A lack of sleep will always create more stress in your life than the amount of work it allows you to accomplish - no matter how much time it does save you for something else.

The power of full nights' rest is often overlooked in today's society, which is why sleeping clinics are popping up around the globe everywhere. Try to take a little time out of your hectic schedule to see if you can find some time to rest. Find a peaceful area and close your eyes for a few minutes, even if it's only for a few minutes. Sleep is not something you want to attempt on an empty stomach. Your mental alertness will be affected as well as your physical performance.

Your level of stress depends on how you are using your energy, but everybody gets stressed out at times - even when they are asleep! If the stress causes your sleep to be interrupted, then it's time to reset yourself. Even small changes in your sleep routine can have a big impact on your stress levels.

When you get enough sleep, you'll feel better and be more productive. By being productive instead of stressed, you will have more time to enjoy the things in life that really matter to you - family, friends and personal hobbies. You can't control how much sleep you get each night but you can control how important it is to remain mindful of it and value it. As with anything else that we do, we must practice making time for rest if we want our bodies and minds to function at their best.

Secret #7: Learn How Stress Affects the Body

Stress causes adrenaline and cortisol to be released into the bloodstream, causing a number of changes in the body. Learn more about these changes here.

We all encounter stress at some point in our life. We shouldn't feel guilty about it -- stress is a normal part of living. The true problem lies in how we handle stress. If we allow our lives to become a stressful mess, then we really have a problem that may affect our health and happiness. We can reduce the amount of stress in our lives by learning to enjoy the little things and making sure we don't let all the negativity around us get to us.

You are likely very familiar with the power of meditation to reduce anxiety, lower your stress levels, and increase positivity. This is because there are many direct correlations between the mind and the body. When you practice mindful meditation your heart rate slows, cortisol levels decline, and negative moods become less intense.

Stress is one of the most common variables that contribute to unhealthy habits such as overeating or binge drinking alcohol, both of which can lead to obesity and alcoholism. Maintaining a cheerful view on life has been proved to be good for our health since it reduces cortisol overproduction, which can lead to weight gain and chronic diseases like cancer and diabetes owing to high insulin levels.

Because stress has a direct effect on our bodies, it's important to understand how to manage your stress as well as how to avoid it as much as possible. Learning about the body's stress response and how the body reacts to stressors allows you to keep your cortisol levels low, without becoming too stressed out about it.

What is Cortisol?

Cortisol is a hormone that helps us cope with stressful situations. It has other names such as hydrocortisone, cortisone, and corticosterone depending on the type of animal. In humans it's often called the "stress hormone".

It is a glucocorticoid which means that it stimulates the production of blood sugar and other energy sources needed to deal with stress. It also affects other functions in the body such as suppressing the immune system or encouraging fat deposition. This is why it's so easy to gain weight from excess cortisol levels, especially around your middle.

In order to create cortisol your body needs a molecule known as pregnenolone which is a steroid produced by a gland in your brain known as the adrenal cortex. It's often called "adrenal hormones" since they are produced from the adrenal glands. Pregnenolone is converted into cortisone which is what your body uses to create cortisol.

Why Does stress Increase Cortisol Levels?

Stress, which is one of the most common triggers, causes cortisol levels to rise. When you're stressed, your body produces adrenaline into your bloodstream, which is designed to assist you deal with the danger. This increases heart rate and blood pressure, increases blood sugar levels for energy, and gets you breathing faster so you can run away! After the stressful situation (e.g. getting chased by a wild animal) is over, your body relaxes your heart rate, lowers blood pressure, and stops breathing so fast.

Problems only start to occur when you are exposed to stress on a regular basis. Your body starts to get used to the adrenaline rush that comes with stressful situations. Adrenaline levels in your body never fall below normal anymore. This means that in every day situations you're always at risk of heart disease or hypertension.

As cortisol gets added to the mix, it starts out by helping you deal with stress in small amounts like running away from a wild animal or dealing with an aggressive co-worker who was rude to you for no reason. It helps you put these kinds of situations into perspective so that they don't have a crippling effect on your life.

The problem comes when you're constantly dealing with stress. Your body gets used to the cortisol rush it gets every time your boss yells at you for no reason or every time your spouse makes an unreasonable demand of you. Your body becomes accustomed to responding to stressors in this manner.

But eventually, it outgrows its regular production of cortisol and starts overproducing it because the daily adrenaline rushes become "normal" for your body. When this happens, cortisol levels are always high which leads to weight gain as well as untreatable diseases like cancer or diabetes.

How can you Tell if your Cortisol is Too High?

The simple answer is that there isn't a good way to measure your cortisol levels outside of a lab. You can, however, monitor the symptoms of elevated cortisol levels. Common symptoms that occur when you have elevated cortisol levels include:

- Depression or sadness that doesn't go away even when you try to think about happy memories.

- Weight gain around your belly which can be an indication of high insulin levels caused by elevated cortisol. This fat tends to be more brown than white fat indicating that it is more dangerous for your health than subcutaneous fat which has a different composition.

- Cellulite which is closely related to insulin resistance. This is why it's important for you to exfoliate frequently (especially in the shower) and use products like Apple Cider Vinegar to help reduce cellulite.

- Lack of libido. When you're stressed, cortisol can overpower testosterone, lowering your sex drive and lowering testosterone production in both men and women. Excessive cortisol can also suppress dopamine levels which are associated with positive moods, motivation, and energy. When dopamine levels are low it's easier to feel depressed or unmotivated.

- Weight Gain around the belly. High cortisol can cause fat to be deposited in an area of your body where there is already excess subcutaneous fat.

- Difficulty Sleeping because you are physically tired due to increased levels of adrenaline and cortisol. Chronic stress can also increase production of melatonin which makes it difficult for your body to fall asleep at night. Melatonin production is suppressed during stress which means that you'll wake up earlier than normal.

- Increased anxiety or lack of motivation after experiencing chronically high cortisol levels for an extended period of time. Chronic stress can make you feel fatigued, moody, and jittery even if you're not overtired. This can make it difficult to focus on your work or feel motivated to exercise.

- Increased blood pressure. Because of high cortisol levels, this can happen when you're stressed. This is why you shouldn't take blood pressure medication if you're experiencing chronic stress.

- Depression caused by abnormal circadian cycles which are regulated by melatonin production possibly caused by high cortisol levels. Melatonin production is suppressed during stress which means that your body works about 4 hours less than it should per day due to the fact that melatonin levels are suppressed instead of increased at night when you need them most.

These symptoms are all signs that you have elevated cortisol levels and it's time to decrease the amount of stress in your life.

How to Reduce Stress and Cortisol Levels Naturally?

The best way to reduce high cortisol levels is by decreasing the amount of stress you have in your life. This isn't always possible because our stressful jobs and demanding home lives don't allow us much free time to take a vacation from reality. The good news is that cortisol levels can be reduced naturally by decreasing the amount of norepinephrine that's being produced.

Norepinephrine is a chemical which has an impact on stress levels. It's responsible for increased heart rate, increased blood pressure, and constriction of blood vessels. These are all symptoms which are considered to be part of the fight or flight mechanism that helps you to deal with stressful situations.

Fighting or fleeing from a stressful situation raises norepinephrine levels. When the stressful situation is over norepinephrine levels should fall back to baseline levels quickly because your body can handle stress on its own without any assistance from stress hormones like cortisol.

However, many people are constantly dealing with chronic stress thanks to their demanding jobs or homes lives. There's always a fight going on in their minds which causes norepinephrine to stay elevated. This is the reason why many doctors prescribe beta blockers to people who are dealing with high blood pressure caused by stress related activities like public speaking, public transportation, or high speed motor vehicle use (this includes motorcycles and motor boats).

The problem is that beta blockers aren't good for you over an extended period of time because they can cause your heart to slow down and contribute to heart failure. The solution is to decrease the amount of norepinephrine in your body and decrease cortisol levels because norepinephrine and cortisol interact with each other.

Cortisol is produced in the adrenal glands when norepinephrine levels are high. This means that when you decrease your norepinephrine levels it's also possible to decrease your cortisol levels which will help you to deal with stress better by yourself. This doesn't mean that you should avoid dealing with stressful situations, but it does mean that you shouldn't deal with them on a daily basis or for days on end which can cause uncontrollable anxiety attacks.

The problem lies with many poor lifestyle choices like poor diet, lack of sleep, and lack of exercise. These may not seem like they are directly affecting your stress levels because they don't cause adrenaline rushes like driving in traffic. However, they still raise your norepinephrine levels which is causing you to feel stressed. The solution is to make positive changes to your lifestyle and reduce stress levels by decreasing the amount of norepinephrine that's being produced.

How to Decrease Norepinephrine Levels

I recommend making a conscious effort to reduce the amount of stress you have in your life by increasing the length of time between stressful events. This doesn't mean that you should avoid any situations that cause stress, but it does mean that you should try to handle them as quickly as possible without getting upset. This helps you to reduce the intensity of stress and allows you to recover faster. If you're running late for work, for example, you should strive to get into the workplace as soon as possible so that you can cope with difficult situations swiftly.

Secret #8: Have a Contingency Plan

Contingency plans have been around for ages and have taken on a more important form in recent years. The goal of a contingency plan is to have a back-up plan in the event that your primary strategy fails. However, this type of situation is not the only example of contingency plans in existence. In order to eliminate stress, you can create your own contingency plan that will help you continue with life without worry each day. The key to creating a contingency plan is to create a plan that can last you for an extended period of time. This is your contingency plan. It will provide you with the ability to carry on without stress during any situation throughout your life. The first step in creating your contingency plan is to remain calm and focused so that any stress has less of an effect on you. Next, the first thing that the contingency plan should contain is an escape clause. An escape clause means that there is some form of backup or another plan that you can use if the situation gets worse than expected. However, this does not mean that there are two plans; it means one single contingency, but one secondary plan as well. The next step is to create the entire contingency plan.

This plan should include everything that you can possibly think of in relation to the situation, while remaining calm and rational. Take some time to think of what situations may be stressful for you or your family. The last step in creating your contingency plan is to identify yourself with your contingency plan. This means that you must remember to use your plan in order for it to remain successful. This will assist you in applying preventive measures against stress before they become major problems or disasters. All this does is set up a strategy that will give you the best possible chance against stress; it does not guarantee that everything will go right. However, if you stick to your plan, chances are that it will work out.

Contingency plans can be used for many different situations throughout life. One contingency plan that everyone should have is an emergency evacuation plan that allows you to flee the area of danger if needed. This type of contingency plan is important no matter the situation; whether you are trapped in a fire or simply need to find another way out of an area. All it takes is some thought and time to create this contingency plan. The key thing about this contingency plan is that it must be one specific emergency evacuation, so it must fit your situation perfectly. As you make your plan, keep this in mind. A general evacuation plan such as "call 911" is not satisfactory. A good example of a proper evacuation plan is "If there is a fire in my house, I will first grab my children and go out the front door. I will then call 911 from the neighbor's house."

This type of plan gives you a clear idea of how to react, while also giving you an escape route should your first method fail. So, before you ever place yourself in any situation where emergency planning may be necessary, make sure to take the time to create a contingency plan that will help you get through it without becoming too stressed or emotionally involved.

Secret #9: Remember You've Been There Before

It would be much easier to manage with stress if we just experienced one minor nuisance per day, but sadly, many of us have a constant stream of stressful situations. When it seems like the weight of the world is pushing you down, sometimes it helps to remember that you've been there before, and you can do it again.

This book will discuss how recalling memories from past experiences can help reduce current stress because remembering an event helps reduce its emotional intensity. By recollecting memories from times where we were able to manage our increased breathing and heart rate due to an intense situation, we can remember that though any situation may feel dire at first glance, overcoming this challenge is within our capabilities.

Once you remember you've handled similar situations in the past, it becomes easier to recognize that you can do so again. Realizing that there are few, if any, issues in life that you haven't dealt with before is comforting because it means that your current challenge is not an insurmountable barrier.

The memories invoked by recalling times where we've overcome challenging situations in the past helps us reduce their emotional intensity by tying them to events with either positive or neutral emotions. This process is called "desensitization." When we feel more relaxed, we can think more clearly about how to deal with the current situation and respond appropriately.

Dr. Johannes Westphal, a German psychiatrist, first proposed that emotional anxiety could be reduced by recalling memories with a different emotional valence in 1914. He found that recalling memories from situations with a larger emotional impact helped patients feel less anxious during their therapy sessions.

Numerous studies since then have demonstrated similar findings for a range of stressful settings, such as public speaking and exam taking scenarios. Dr. Stephen D. Phillips, a psychologist at Northwestern University, has repeatedly verified Westphal's findings in his own research with memory recall as the key to reducing anxiety.

When discussing how memories can act as a coping mechanism during stressful situations, Dr. Phillips describes memory recall as "a kind of psychological 'vaccine' that inoculates people against the debilitating effects of stress by helping them remember that they have coped with this type of situation before."

Dr. Phillips and his colleagues found that patients who recalled positive memories such as learning a new skill had physiological responses that closely resembled those of people who were not stressed at all. These patients exhibited lower blood pressure, higher heart rates, and lower rates of oxygen consumption compared to people with neutral memories. By recalling happy experiences, they were able to feel less emotional anxiety about their current circumstance.

Even if you're not used to recalling traumatic events from the past, it's crucial to realize that you can do so right now. Every day, set aside a few minutes to reflect about good occurrences from your past—a nice trip, lunch with old friends—and how you handled them previously.

During daily stressors, take a minute to recall any happy memories that may be currently triggering. Even if you can't remember exactly how you dealt with similar situations in the past, just knowing that you have experienced them before will allow you to feel more at ease now.

By noticing your breathing and heart rate, and remembering that they were both under control during past stressful situations, it becomes easier for you to realize that your current stressful situation is not outside of your capabilities. When we remember we've been through these types of experiences before and survived, we know we can do it again.

Secret #10: Listen to Music

If you're feeling stressed and overwhelmed, the best thing you can do is take a deep breath and listen to music. Music has been proven to combat stress-related health problems and improve your mood, so it's a great way to start feeling better in no time!

Music can be an incredibly potent tool for de-stressing and elevating moods. These days, we're living on fast food, advertisements, and workaholic schedules that leave little time for nature or personal reflection.

A little quiet time can help you get in touch with your body's rhythms, enhance the effects of other relaxation techniques, and reduce stress levels.

The Benefits of Music

1. Sound Waves Have Healing Powers

As you know, music has always had the ability to heal the body. The vibrations that are emitted from instruments help purify energy in the body and relieve stress in many ways. It's for this reason that musicians often wear earplugs while playing in concert halls. Hearing loss is an occupational hazard for musicians, but using musical instruments helps prevent hearing loss because it stimulates the inner ear and keeps it healthy.

2. Music Can Increase the Brain's Pain-Relieving Response

The brain releases natural opioids when you get injured or injured. These natural painkillers are known as endorphins and they come in the form of tiny chemical particles called neurotransmitters. When researchers played music for rats to listen to, they found that the sound waves increased the amount of endorphins in their bodies which helped ease pain levels. If you're battling chronic pain or just want to get rid of it for good, this is a great option to consider.

3. Sleep Can Be Easier With Music

Sound waves have a soothing effect on the mind and body. The sound waves you hear stimulate your brain, which relaxes your muscles and helps you fall asleep faster. You don't have to listen to music when you go to bed in order to get a good night's rest. Instead, try listening before going to sleep so that your brain can get the same benefit from the sound waves from music.

4. Music Provides a Natural High

The power of music is pretty amazing, and you can take this for granted as long as you live. The sound waves from music have been known to have a euphoric effect on the mind, body, and even emotions. In fact, you can feel a natural high by just humming a tune under your breath.

Music has been shown to alleviate anxiety and deliver a welcome boost.

5. Music Releases Endorphins Into the Body

Endorphins are chemical substances that have pain-relieving properties in the body. They're vital for your physical health because they allow you to feel good without having to use any narcotics or medications. Music is a great way to get these endorphins flowing because it puts you in a natural state of mind that makes you happy and improves your outlook on life.

6. Music Has a Relaxing Effect On the Mind and Body

The sound waves from instruments cause a reaction in the body that's similar to the way you react to an injury. When you're exposed to music, your body produces serotonin which helps ease depression, relaxes your muscles, and makes you experience less stress throughout the day. Music can even help reduce stress-related health problems like headaches and migraines.

7. Music Reduces Appetite

When you're feeling hungry, it can be hard to stay focused on productive tasks. Music is known to suppress the appetite and help you eat less. If you're looking to lose weight or just want to stop eating so much, this is a great way to do it. All you have to do now is turn on the music and dance!

8. Music Improves Your Mood

When you're sad or depressed, everything seems worse than usual. It's remarkable how quickly music can change your mood without making you feel as if something is amiss with your life or that something is terribly wrong with your thinking. Music can really change your state of mind in this way because it's very powerful in what it does to the brain.

9. Music Can Help You Focus Better

Being able to focus on something when you're feeling overwhelmed is a great way to feel better when you're ready for it. Music helps you become more productive because you're able to focus in a way that's much easier for your body and mind.

10. Music is Good Mental Exercise

As far as exercise goes, music is considered a form of physical exercise because your body needs to move to hear the sounds coming from the instruments. It's for this reason that you can reduce fat without actually moving by listening to music.

11. Music Improves Your Immune System

Your immune system gets weaker when you're struggling with illness or depression, which is why music can help keep your body strong. Sound waves from your favorite songs' instruments stimulate hormones in your body that protect it from harm and build your immune system, allowing you to fight illnesses and diseases much more effectively than before.

12. Music Helps Fight Depression

When you're sad, it can be difficult to overcome on your own because stress tends to exacerbate the situation.

Music is great for getting over depression because it helps you relax and makes you feel happier.

13. Music Can Help Fight Attention Deficit Disorder

Millions of children and adults suffer with attention deficit hyperactivity disorder (ADHD). It's a disorder that makes it difficult for people to concentrate on something, especially if the person has trouble focusing on what he or she is doing. Music can help because it's characterized by being very rhythmic which helps improve concentration in many people with ADHD.

14. Music Helps You Stay Healthy Risk-Free

The benefits of music don't stop there because it can offer you some protection from the effects of many diseases, illnesses, and health conditions. There are many things you can do to improve your physical and emotional health, including listening to music that might help you cope with stress or despair.

15. Music Reduces Symptoms of ADD and ADHD

If you're suffering from ADHD, music can help you in the following ways:

Helps with staying focused Replenishes energy levels Makes it easier to concentrate and pay attention Helps to improve academic performance in students with ADHD.

Secret #11: Minimize Distractions

Being distracted all the time can be really frustrating. It's like the more you try to work, the less you get done. Why is that? Well, it's because distractions aren't just inconvenient; they're also sabotaging your work ethic and your productivity! Actually, people may not even realize how much stress distracters are causing until they experiment with eliminating them. Consider this: researchers found that even though people who were distracted were doing their tasks slower than those who weren't distracted at all, subjects still felt less stressed when being distracted by something unrelated to their current assignment.

So, really, it's important to realize that a distraction is a real drain on your concentration and time management ability. It can literally stop you from getting anything done at all or it can literally bring you to the edge of giving up altogether – both of which simply aren't good ideas. So if you find yourself feeling really stressed out and overwhelmed because of distractions, it's time to take action and rid yourself of them as much as possible!

As an example, let's say that your boss keeps interrupting your work with phone calls. It's important to ask your boss, on your next meeting, if there's another way he/she can contact you in case of emergencies. Then you'll need to find another way to contact him or her, such as sending an e-mail or texting. Or, even better, if it's possible, ask your boss for a voicemail so he/she can leave you voice messages when there's an emergency and you're not around. If it seems like your boss isn't on board with this idea so far, it may be best to bring up the benefits of fewer distractions from work for both parties. If you really want a voicemail, there's a good chance your boss will agree in the end.

You can also minimize distractions in real life by not having your cell phone on you when you're doing work. A study conducted in 2008 showed that subjects who were interrupted by a ringing cell phone took longer to finish their task than those who weren't interrupted at all. This is because of how quickly the ringing of the cell phone distracts us and how it makes us feel obligated to respond right away even if we don't want to. If you're just trying to get your work done and your cell phone keeps ringing, it's best not even having it on you while doing so, and instead check it every hour or so.

Moreover, if you really want to block out distractions in general, try using a pair of noise-canceling headphones. Many offices have them and I used them when I worked in an office setting. They're great for blocking out chatter from co-workers because they literally cancel out the sounds around you. In fact, it feels like you're not even in the same room as anyone else! They're great for getting work done without having to hear all the distractions around you.

In addition, don't put yourself in places where there are many distractions from work. This means avoiding places where there are lots of people, especially if you're focusing on something that requires a lot of concentration. If you need to go to the library or some other place where you know there's generally not many distractions, do it. If you're at home and want to get stuff done, do it in the room that's the least noisy and has the least distractions.

If you're feeling overwhelmed or anxious at work, your best bet is to make changes as soon as possible by eliminating as many distractions as possible. You'll feel better after doing so!

Secret #12: Call Someone

Imagine you've just been dealt a rude blow: your degree doesn't seem to be worth much after all, and you rack up $30,000 of student debt in the process. Or maybe it's the end of your relationship; all your efforts at making your partner happy have come to naught. Stress is an emotion that can eat away at you like a cancer, and nobody cures it like talking to someone who can help. It might be tough to de-stress yourself with self-therapy — but there's no doubt that human contact is beneficial for mental health and contentment.

When you're stressed out, you're locked in a cycle of negative feelings. You feel anxious, upset, angry, or frustrated. These emotions are often compounded with depression , the feeling that your situation's hopeless. Just being aware of these deleterious states can make you feel worse. And so begins the cycle: You feel stressed because you're anxious and depressed, so you think about it more... and more ... and more... and it never ends.

This is why talking to someone is the best medicine: talking to someone is like opening a window and allowing fresh air to come inside – it allows new thoughts and emotions to enter your mind, giving them room to breathe. It would be even better if you could speak with a psychologist, but this is typically too expensive. The best alternative for stress alleviation is typically a friend or family member.

The problem is that there's a reason why people don't reach out to others when they're stressed: they might feel ashamed of their problems, or think that nobody cares. Putting yourself in their position and seeing if you can understand where they're coming from is the greatest method to start them talking. Ask them what they think about things and how they approach life: this will help them open up and give you something else to talk about other than the problem at hand. Learn from the ordeal and move on. Learn from their mistakes and move on. That's how you improve yourself – not by looking back, but looking forward.

Everyone has stressful situations: like a bad grade, a tax bill, or a fight with an ex. There's nothing wrong with letting those things affect you; after all, we can't control what other people do. And it's good to see the world outside of our immediate environment: it can make us more aware of our situation and help us cope better with the problems we face every day.

But that doesn't imply we should be affected by everything. We all face hardships, and we should be able to deal with them – but it's important to understand our strengths and weaknesses. Don't let things build up; take benefits from each experience and learn from it.

Remember, there's no such thing as a problem that can't be solved: there are problems you can't solve, and problems you can solve. They don't all need to be tackled head-on –

sometimes the best thing we can do is to take a step back, watch our experiences – and move on – without hurting ourselves or others – just as we hope others will do for us.

When we experience stress, our body and mind react to these physical and mental pressures in a negative way. This can lead to problems such as physical harm, impaired decision making, and even depression.

But there is a solution. There are ways of decreasing your stress levels through mindful introspection and social engagement - such as meditation or calling someone you care for during times of difficulty. And while it may seem counterintuitive to rely on another person during times of difficulty, the benefits outweigh the risks: When we contact another human being to talk about how they're doing in their lives or share an anecdote about your day in yours, it releases endorphins in our brain that trigger a sense of happiness and well-being.

The benefits of a good conversation include:

- Eliminating stress and anxiety.
- Lessening depression by helping us understand our feelings.
- Increasing social bonds with the people we care about the most.
- Allowing us to be more empathetic towards others.
- Helping us make sense of our place in the world through self-reflection and reflection on the world at large.
- Giving us a chance to recharge after a long day or week of work or study.

- Stimulating the formation of new friendships by initiating conversations.
- Giving us a chance to practice our social skills.

And these are all reasons why, rather than surfing the internet or watching television, you should utilize your time properly to make phone calls.

But there are also some unfortunate side effects to making phone calls during times of stress, namely that most people react negatively when you call them. They may be annoyed, think it's rude, or feel anxious because they are afraid they don't have enough time for you. But if you become more empathetic and realize that their negative attitude is the result of imbalanced levels of stress, they will be more willing to help you with your problems.

Conclusion

Stress is a tricky thing. It's good for some things, like helping you to mobilize the fight-or-flight response in dangerous situations, but it can also be disastrous for your health otherwise.

The good news is that it's possible to make stress your friend! We've compiled a list of our best stress-relieving techniques, along with instructions on how to incorporate them into your daily routine. They're especially helpful when you're feeling bogged down by anxiety or suddenly feel stressed out by an everyday situation.

So grab your favorite beverage, take a breath, and get ready to read some life-changing secrets!

Triggering is another method for creating new behaviors in the brain.

A trigger is anything that triggers the behavior you're trying to change. Triggers can be biological (such as when you feel hungry), learned (such as when you think about something that makes you happy), or due to your environment (such as when you walk into a familiar place). Once you identify these triggers, it's time to work on changing how the behavior happens so they aren't so automatic anymore.

The prime example of this is avoidance. You might want to avoid a stressful situation, but it's hard to do while you're in the middle of it. Instead, find ways to trigger yourself into changing behavior before you get there.

One way is to imagine how your life will improve once the stress is gone! Fight or flight may be appropriate for some situations, but even here there are alternatives. You can pursue other behaviors that will help you feel better once the danger is over. For example, try relaxation techniques before anxiety becomes overwhelming so you can take care of yourself instead of being overwhelmed by something that shouldn't have happened in the first place.

Many people have trouble with this because they assume that if they don't want something to happen, it must happen anyway. And it's true: no matter what you think or believe, the world will continue to turn.

Meditation and yoga, for example, can assist you in breaking free from that cycle by allowing you to gain control over your body and mind. You can also do things like taking a walk or calling a friend when anxiety is starting to get the better of you. Little things can make a big difference!

Being able to relax is an important part of changing your perspective on life. If we're always worried about our problems and how we can best solve them, we'll also be more stressed than ever. So it's important to learn to look at situations differently.

Taking a break, whether it's time out in nature, having a coffee with a friend, or spending time with your significant other, helps to reset your perspective. You'll be able to see things from someone else's perspective - with less stress!

There are also things you may do right now to alleviate your pain. For example, taking deep breaths when you start feeling overwhelmed (sometimes called "belly breathing") can help relax the body and reduce anxiety in the mind. You can also try visualizing in your head that there is only one problem that needs solving in this situation - nothing more and nothing less.

When there's something that annoys you, take a moment to focus on what brings you the most pleasure. The things that make you happy are by definition those things that bring you less stress! So remind yourself of those things when you feel stressed, and look for ways to incorporate them into your life. You can even take things like Netflix and video games and put them on pause so they aren't stressing your life out for no reason. Change them up!

One easy way to stop automatically doing annoying habits is to physically stop yourself from doing them. For example, if you bite your nails, force yourself to bite on a pencil instead. If you're one of those people that blows into the holes in the lid of a bottle when there's no more soda left, just don't do it!

We can become so engrossed in the patterns we've established that we don't even notice we're performing them. Rather than fighting it, find methods to avoid these bothersome behaviors with simple tricks like holding your breath before saying something you know would offend someone - this allows wisdom to take over and prevent an argument.

There are a lot of things that can cause stress. We may have a job we don't like, a relationship that isn't going well, an impending deadline at work, or a lot of other things.

And sometimes we're in the middle of a stressful situation and need a way to change our behavior when help from outside aren't available.

But it's not all bad news! As you've learned from reading this book, it's possible to reduce stress in your life by changing your behavior with things like trigger identification and relaxation techniques. You can also change your mind by changing your perspective or switching up your routines.

So what are you waiting for? Change the way you respond to difficult events and how you connect with the rest of the world. Better yet, change yourself from the inside! When you lead by example, the world will be a better place!

We gradually become what we repeatedly think. Hence, self-improvement is really self-creation. In other words, if we want to improve ourselves (and therefore our lives), we need to create ourselves in our own image - to make ourselves who we want to be right now.

If you're frequently exposed to stressful situations, adrenaline can be difficult to manage and can cause a headache all on its own. The good news is that there are ways that you can reduce your levels of stress without being stuck with all of those pesky symptoms of anxiety and panic attacks- just by making some minor changes within your life! Here are some useful hints that will reduce your anxiety and allow you to live a more pleasant life:

1) Start living slowly.

Slowing down is one of the quickest strategies to control your adrenaline. By living in an rushed, stressful manner, you are constantly telling your body that it needs to be in fight or flight mode.

2) Keep a journal.

Keeping a journal is always a great way for people who suffer from panic attacks and stress- there are just so many benefits! It will also help you to see what has gone on recently so you can adjust your schedule so you aren't faced with the same mental breakdown over and over again.

3) Stop using harmful techniques.

There are some things that your body responds to so strongly, not only that they can cause anxiety but can actually make it worse. Taking medicine on a daily basis, smoking cigarettes or even drinking alcohol all affect the shape of your brain and therefore cause stress. If you feel like you're already stressed out, don't make it worse by numbing your body with these substances or chemicals- they won't help!

4) Set realistic goals.

Are you a perfectionist? Perfection is probably the number one reason for all of those stress related breakdowns. When you have a few things to achieve done in a short period of time, it is inevitable that you will be stressed out and anxious over it. Not only that, but if you set small goals for yourself with a decent amount of time to achieve them in, there will be no reason to worry so much!

5) Talk about your feelings.

By talking about what you're feeling, you can reduce or eliminate stress- not just because it gives your body a release but because deep down, you want to know all of those things about yourself. Talking to people about your feelings and thoughts allows you to see things in a more typical light and takes your attention off of whatever is bothering you.

6) Watch less television.

Turn off your television, especially if it is on constantly. Watching television can cause your emotions to skyrocket, especially when you feel like the characters are in danger. Watching TV doesn't give you much time to think about what is happening around you, what you're feeling in reality or what shows are on lately! If the only thing that is happening in your life is television, you won't be able to see much else.

7) Are you constantly worrying?

If the answer is yes, then there may be some things happening in your life that aren't exactly ideal. Instead of worrying about these things, just scan your life for any areas that you are stressed out about. Are you worried about your job? Classes? Is there something else in life that is bothering you? If so, try to change it.

8) Look at things in a different light.

When things are worrying you, try to see the good in them! A positive mind only takes so much stress, so when your mind is focusing on the bad side of things, look at the positives instead! It may not be easy but looking at the positive is a great way for your brain to feel calm and relaxed. Not only that, but when you see things in a better light, they'll be more likely to turn out well for you!

9) Turn to your friends and family.

There is no one better than your best friend or significant partner to chat to when you need someone to talk to. Not only is it great for your mental health but it will also help you see things in a different light- and can even help you feel more comfortable about telling them how you feel. Not only that, but the people who love us the most are usually very good at detecting panic attacks and we can get them before we get too stuck in our emotions.

10) Take a bath.

Taking a bath is one of the most luxurious experiences that you can have, especially if it isn't something that you're used to doing on a regular basis- not only does it help to relax your body but you can also put your mind at ease as well.

11) Keep stress relievers with you at all times.

Stress release tools are great to have with you when life gets stressful because they help keep your mind settled and relaxed. Not only that, but they are good at helping you not get too worked up when you are in stressful situations. You can even keep these tools in your car so that when you're on the road, you can just rub them with your fingers and help yourself to feel better.

12) Make small changes in your life.

Do you buy your food at the same place every time? Try buying something different! If you don't like what it is, then go back to what you like! Not only will introducing new items to your body be beneficial to your health, but it will also keep things exciting for you.

13) Don't hold in your emotions.

If you keep things to yourself, it can cause a lot of stress in your life. Not only that, but when you keep things bottled up for too long, they can be hard to burst out and sometimes make more sense when they seem silly or weird when you do finally let them go. Therefore, try not to hold things in and talk about them with others!

14) Take the time to meditate.

Meditating is one of the best ways to keep your stress down to a minimum. Not only will you feel more relaxed but you also will be more balanced and calm. While it may seem impossible, even if you practice for 10 minutes a day, it can make a huge difference in your life!

Meditation is a great way for you to relieve stress but also help with everything else as well. Not only does it help you to relax, but you are able to clear your mind. Not only that, but meditation is important because not only does it release endorphins which make you happy but it also helps to get rid of toxins and even lower blood pressure.

15) Exercise!

Exercising is an incredible way for you to be able to deal with stress better than ever. When you exercise, it not only releases endorphins into your body but it also makes your brain happy as well! Not only that, but when you exercise, it releases something called serotonin which is supposed to keep depression away.

16) Ditch the caffeine and soda.

When you're stressed out and anxious and trying to get through your day, coffee or soda may seem like the best thing in the world for you. Well, they aren't! A great way to relieve stress is to make sure that you get a good night of sleep and don't eat too much of anything until you get a lot of rest. When you go on little periods of sleep, coffee or soda are usually the only things that would help you relax.

17) Try holistic treatments.

Holistic treatments, which are natural answers for many medical ailments as well as stress alleviation, are a terrific approach to relieve stress. When you use something that is all-natural, you are less likely to have any bizarre side effects or have to worry about anything that could have come from synthetic medicine.

18) Don't think of yourself as fragile.

Never think of yourself as being too fragile to handle things on your own. You can take care of yourself without depending on anyone else. Not only that, but you will be better off when no one is depending on you for anything!

19) Laugh every now and again!

Laughing helps to release stress and also can ease your worries. When you laugh, it helps to release adrenaline and endorphins which are very good for your body. For this reason, laughter can be a wonderful way to calm down before an emotional situation or to relieve stress during the day!

20) Stop comparing yourself to others.

When we compare ourselves to others, it's simple to become worried. When we do this, it can set us up to be unhappy with ourselves and cause more harm than good. Not only that, but when you compare yourself to others, you may focus on the negative things about yourself and ignore all the positive ones.

21) Stop thinking about things that could go wrong.

When you're stressed, it's easy to imagine all the things that could go wrong, even if they're exceedingly implausible or absurd. If you think of the things that could go wrong, you are likely to put more stress on yourself and make the situation seem more difficult than it actually is.

22) Get rid of your clutter.

While clutter is great for storing things, it can also cause stress in your life. Therefore, it is best if you get rid of your clutter and live a simpler life because it makes everything a lot easier to deal with! When you have less things around you, it becomes a lot easier to relax and have a good time!

23) Go out with friends.

When you go out with friends, it can help you to relieve stress and also to have fun! You'll be able to make jokes with your buddies about the problems you're having. Not only that, but when you go out with friends, you will be able to drink alcohol which is usually one of the most effective ways of relieving yourself of stress.

24) Remember that there is more than one way to relieve stress.

While it may seem as if there is no way for you to relax at all, remember that there are numerous ways to reduce stress without the use of medications or simple techniques. This can even include taking a nice hot bath or meditating. Therefore, don't feel like you have to do more than you can handle!

25) Don't let stress get in the way of your work.

When you're under a lot of stress, it's natural to want to put work aside and just unwind. However, this can make it a lot harder for you to deal with things when you finally have time on your hands! Not only that, but having a lot of work on your plate makes it much more difficult to relax and get rid of tension because your mind will be thinking about even more tasks to complete.

26) Practice mindfulness.

Mindfulness is a fantastic method to deal with stress and can also teach you how to stop thinking negative thoughts. Mindfulness allows you to live in the present moment while also assisting in the release of endorphins, which make you feel better! Not only that, but it can help you become more aware of all of your senses, especially your body which is one of the best ways for you to handle stress better than ever!

27) Watch something funny.

Another great way for you to be able to relieve stress is by watching something funny! When you watch something that is going to make you laugh, it is going to not only help you relax a little bit more but it can also change your mood completely! Not only that, but laughing helps your body release endorphins which makes the whole experience a lot better because then it also gives you a better outlook on things.

28) Cut others some slack.

When you get stressed out, it is easy to get mad at other people who aren't doing anything about your problems. While it's not as if they're attempting to stress you out on purpose, it doesn't mean they should be able to get away with it no matter how many times they do it. Not only that, but the more stress you put on other people, the more things you will have to deal with in your life when they try to mess up your work!

29) Stop worrying so much.

Not only that, but when you worry all the time, it gets very difficult for you to handle. As a result, the more you stress about things that could go wrong, the more likely everything will go wrong and develop into an even bigger disaster.

30) Try to make some new friends.

While it may sound like a very bad idea to try to make friends who stress you out, it can actually help you to relieve stress because then you will be able to talk to them and try to get your mind off of things too. Not only that but when you have new friends who can both relax and also give you advice, it ends up making things so much better because then all of the sudden, things start going your way!

31) Get back into shape.

We tend to gain weight when we are stressed. This is because when we stress, our bodies naturally try to protect us by putting on weight in order to help us survive. When we are stressed, it is simple to eat junk food and not give a damn about our health. This is why it is critical that you exercise and eat well! Our bodies will appreciate you for exercising and getting back into shape!

32) Choose the right time to relieve yourself of stress.

You should know that there are times during the day where it is not a very good idea for you to be stressed out because this can cause a lot of problems for your body. Therefore, when you want to relieve stress, you should do it in the morning when you wake up and before bed at night. This way, you will be able to fall asleep faster and sleep better!

33) Eat healthy food.

Another reason why we put on weight when we are stressed is because we tend to eat junk food and not care about the healthiest things that we can eat. When you eat unhealthy food, it can cause a lot of problems for your body and because of this, you will be stressed out all the time! Therefore, try to eat healthy and put on some muscle mass because it will help you to relax and feel better than ever before.

34) Have a routine.

When we are stressed, it is easier to allow things to control us rather than us controlling them. This is why we should make sure that we have a routine when we relieve ourselves of stress. Having a routine can help you to feel as if everything is going to be okay no matter what happens.

35) Keep stress daily notes.

You may be feeling really stressed out about something that happened in the past. While it is okay to feel this way, it can sometimes be hard for you to get over things if you keep thinking about them. Therefore, when you feel like you are under a lot of stress, try to write down what is making you mad or upset so that you can let these feelings go!

Thank You!

Hope you've enjoyed your reading experience.

So I'd like to thank you for supporting me and reading until the very end.

Before you go, would you mind leaving, a review on Amazon?

It will mean a lot to me and support me in creating high-quality books, for you in the future.

Thanks once again and here's where you can leave a review:

Warmly yours,

Steve V. Meyer

Download Your Free Gift

Before you go any further, why not pick up a gift from us to you?

GROWTH PRINCIPLES

If you're willing to learn and transform yourself in all the right areas,

then success is definitely for you.

So, to find out how you can do that, let's get reading.

Scan the barcode to get it before it expires!

Feel free to continue your journey with us, where you will find new resources, tools, blogs, and advanced notice of new books at…

www.booksandsummaries.com

www.ingramcontent.com/pod-product-compliance
Lightning Source LLC
Chambersburg PA
CBHW072207100526
44589CB00015B/2413